E S T A T E   P U B L

TRURO · FALMOU

CARNON DOWNS · MYLOR BRIDGE
PENRYN · ST MAWES

C000007326

ROAD MAP Pages 2-3

INDEX TO STREETS Pages 14-16

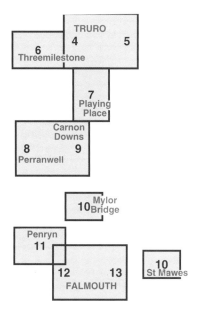

Every effort has been made to verify the accuracy of information in this book but the publishers cannot accept responsibility for expense or loss caused by an error or omission. Information that will be of assistance to the user of the maps will be welcomed.

The representation on these maps of a road, track or path is no evidence of the existence of a right of way.

Car Park	P
Public Convenience	C
Place of Worship	+
One-way Street	→
Pedestrianized	▨
Post Office	●

Scale of street plans 4 inches to 1 mile
Unless otherwise stated

Street plans prepared and published by ESTATE PUBLICATIONS, Bridewell House, TENTERDEN, KENT. The Publishers acknowledge the co-operation of the local authorities of towns represented in this atlas.

Ordnance Survey® This product includes mapping data licensed from Ordnance Survey® with the permission of the Controller of Her Majesty's Stationery Office.

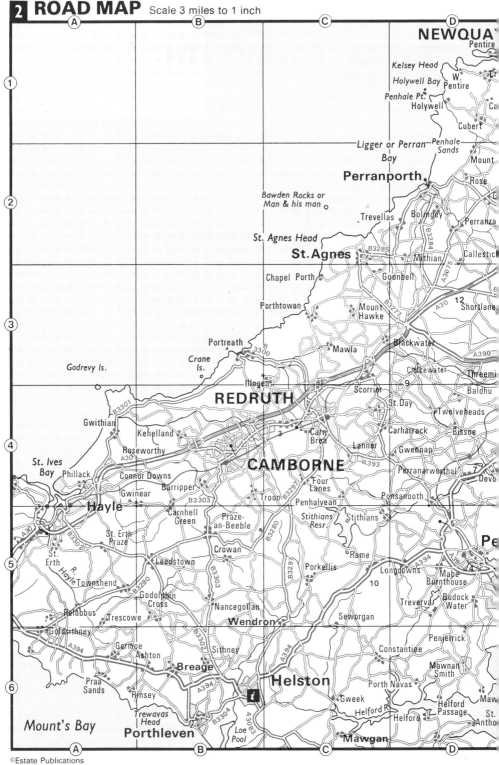

NEWQUA
Pentire

A B C D

1

Kelsey Head
Holywell Bay W
Pentire
Penhale Pt.
Holywell
Cubert

Ligger or Perran
Bay
Penhale
Sands

Mount
Perranporth
Rose
Perranza

2

Bawden Rocks or
Man & his man
Trevellas Bolingey
Perranza
Callestic

St. Agnes Head
St. Agnes
Mithian

B3285 B3284 A3075

Chapel Porth
Goonbell

Porthtown
Mount
Hawke
12
Shortlane

3

Portreath
Mawla
Blackwater
A390

Crane
Is.
Illogan
Scorrier
Chacewater
Threemi

Godrevy Is.
B3300
St. Day
Baldhu

REDRUTH
Twelveheads

Gwithian
Carharrack
Bissoe

Kehelland
Carn
Brea
Lanner
Gwennap

Roseworthy
CAMBORNE
Perranworthal
Devo

4

St. Ives
Bay
Connor Downs
Four
Lanes
Ponsanooth

Phillack
Barripper
Troon
Penhalvean
7

Gwinear
Stithians
Resr.
Stithians

Hayle
B3303
Carnhell
Green
Praze-
an-Beeble
Rame
Longdowns
Mabe
Burnthouse

St. Erth
Praze
Crowan
Porkellis
10
Trevarras
Budock
Water

5

St.
Erth
Leedstown
Pe

Townshend
Godolphin
Cross
Nancegollan
Seworgan

Relubbus
Trescowe
Wendron
Penjerrick

Goldsithney
Constantine

Germoe
Ashton
Sithney
Mawnan
Smith

6

Breage
Porth Navas
Maw

Praa
Sands
Rinsey
Helston
Gweek
Helford
Passage
St.
Antho

Trewavas
Head
Porthleven
Loe
Pool
Mawgan
Helford R
Helford

Mount's Bay

©Estate Publications

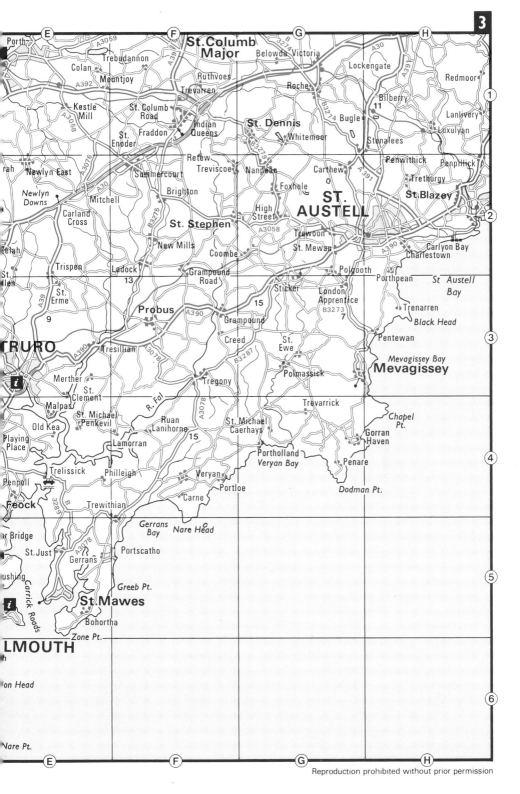

3

E · F · St.Columb · G · H
Major

Porth
Trebudannon
A3059
Belowda Victoria
B4
A30
Colan
Mountjoy
Ruthvoes
Roche
Lockengate
Redmoor
A392
Trevarren
Bilberry
11
Lanlivery
Kestle Mill
St. Columb Road
St. Dennis
B3274
Bugle
Luxulyan
A3058
Fraddon
Indian Queens
Whitemoor
Stenalees
Penwithick
Penpillick
St. Enoder
Retew
Carthew
Trethurgy
rah
Newlyn East
Treviscoe
Nanpean
Foxhole
St. Blazey
Newlyn Downs
Summercourt
Brighton
High Street
ST. AUSTELL
St.Blazey
Mitchell
A30
Carland Cross
St. Stephen
A3058
Trewoon
Carlyon Bay
Zelah
St. Erme
New Mills
Coombe
St. Mewan
Charlestown
Trispen
Ladock
13
Grampound Road
15
Sticker
Polgooth
Porthpean
St Austell Bay
Probus
A390
Grampound
London Apprentice
B3273
7
Trenarren
Black Head
9
Creed
St. Ewe
Pentewan
TRURO
A390
Tresillian
B3078
B3287
Tregony
Polmassick
Mevagissey Bay
Mevagissey
Merther
St. Clement
Malpas
St. Michael Penkevil
Ruan Lanihorne
15
A3078
Trevarrick
Chapel Pt.
Old Kea
St. Michael Caerhays
Gorran Haven
Playing Place
Lamorran
Portholland
Veryan Bay
Penare
Trelissick
Philleigh
Veryan
Dodman Pt.
Penpoll
B3289
Portloe
Feock
Trewithian
Carne
Gerrans Bay
Nare Head
r Bridge
A3078
St.Just
Portscatho
Gerrans
ushing
Greeb Pt.
St.Mawes
Carrick Roads
Bohortha
LMOUTH
Zone Pt.
on Head

Nare Pt.

E · F · G · H

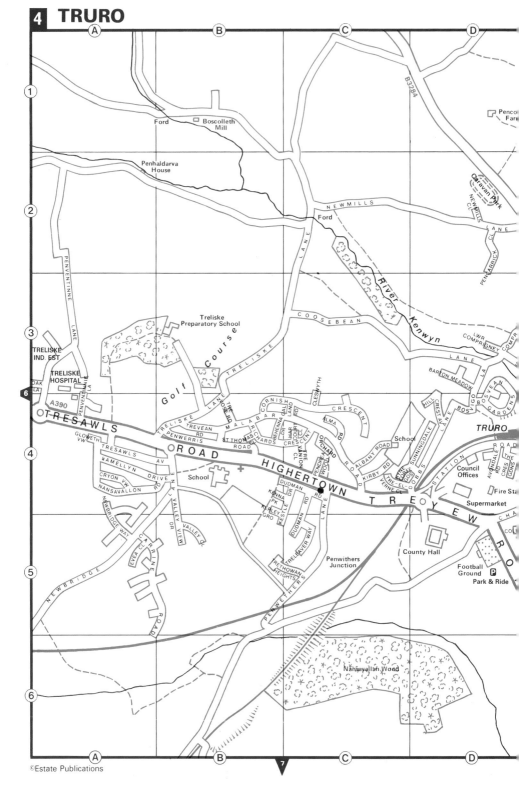

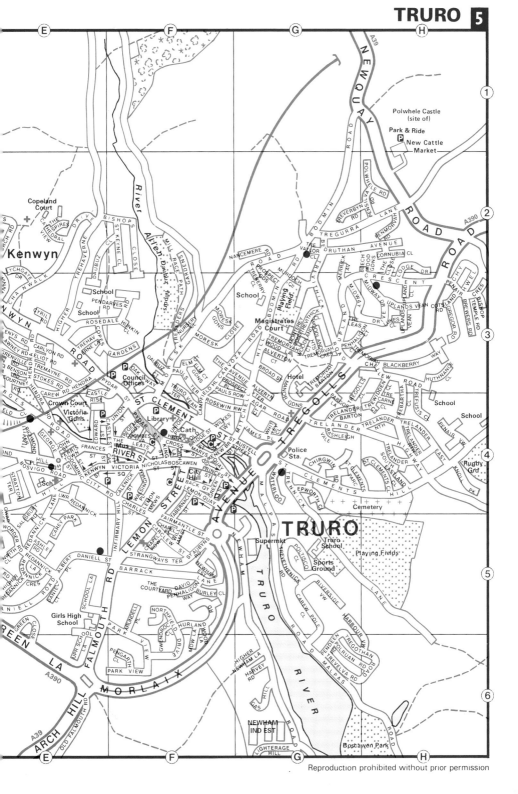

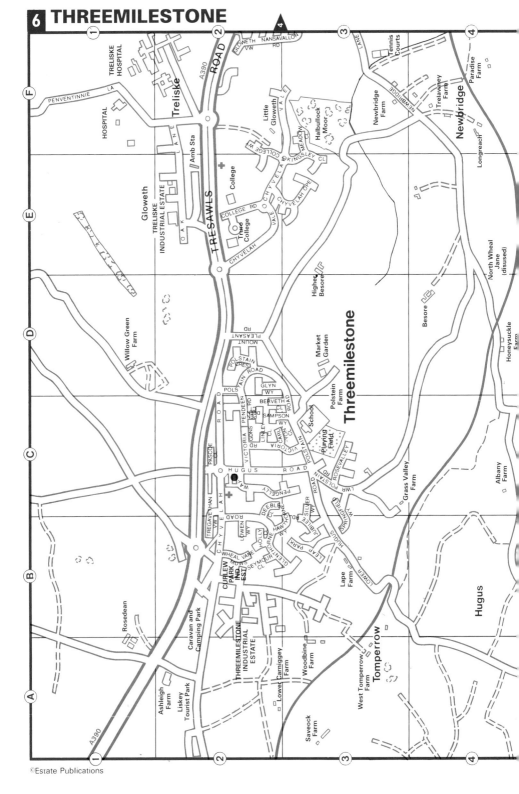

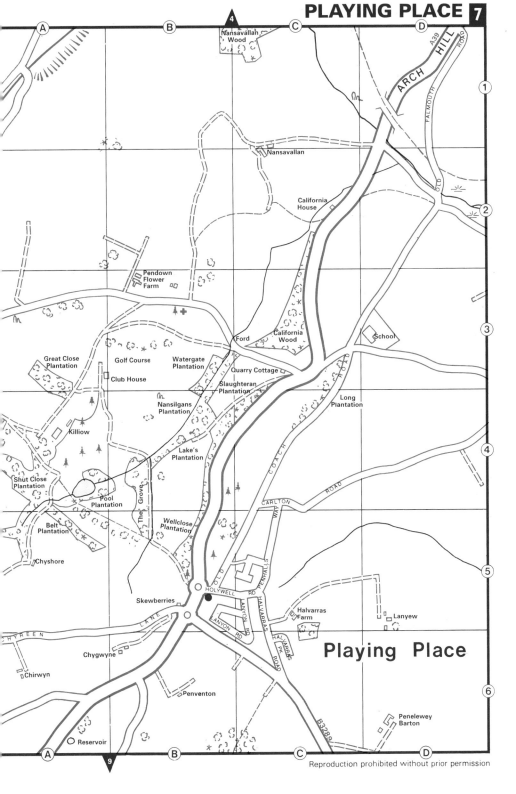

Playing Place

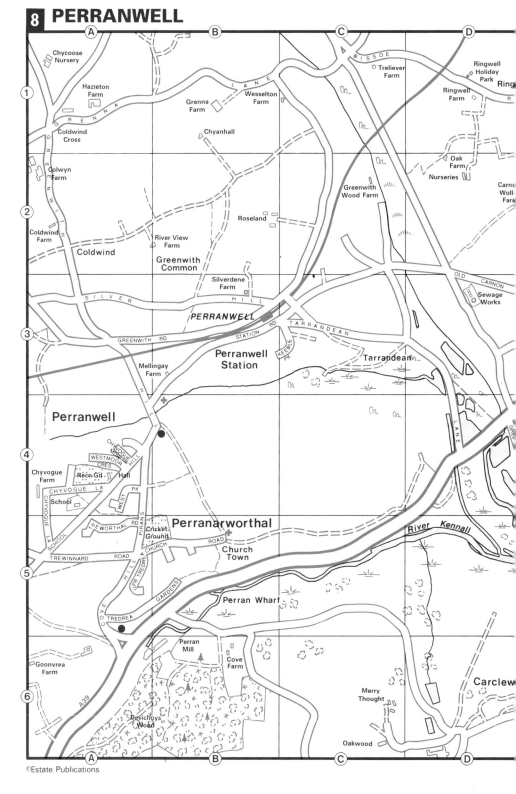

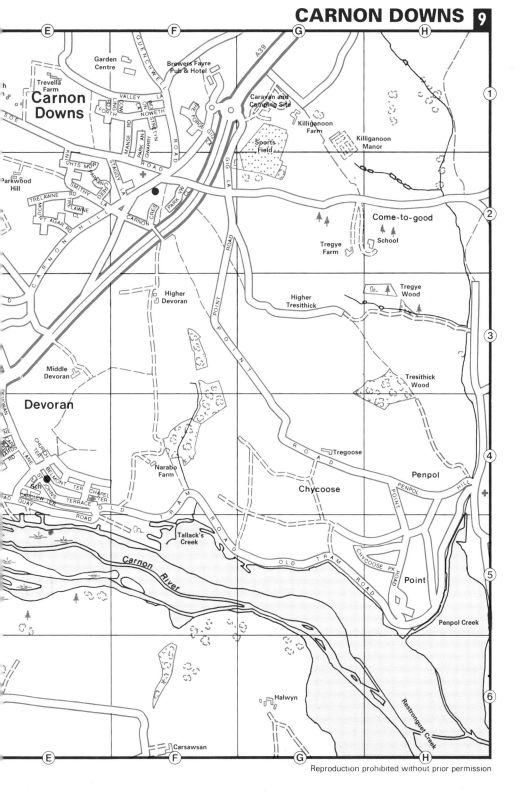

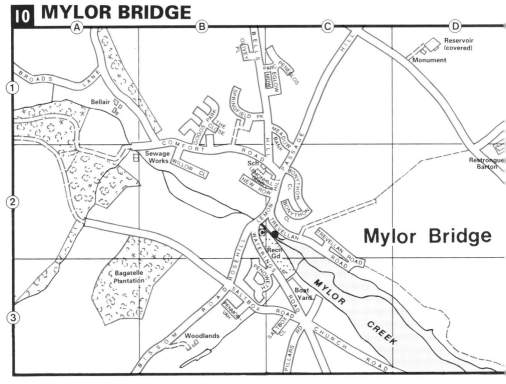

ST. MAWES

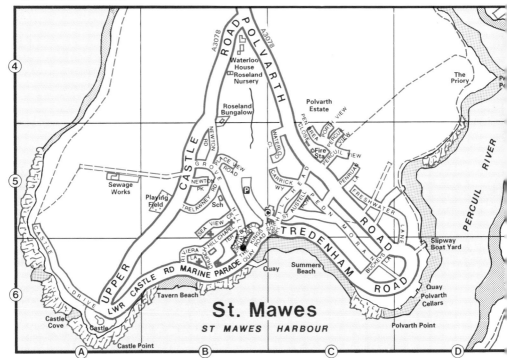

©Estate Publications

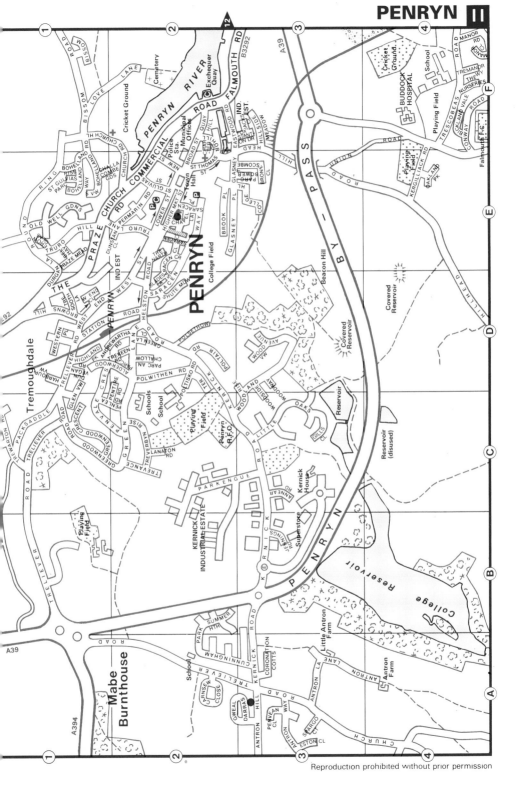

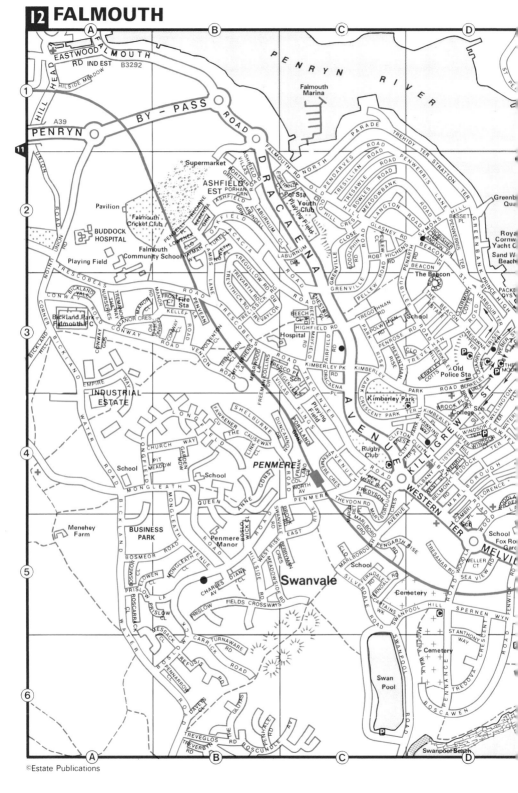

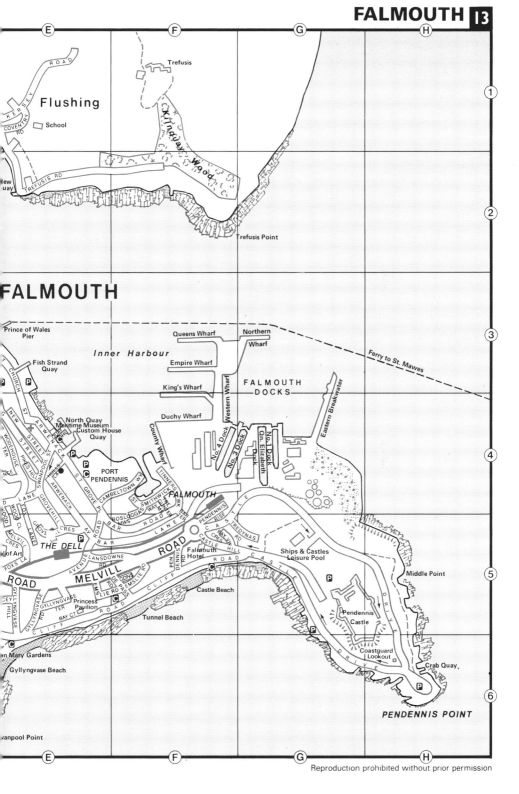

Trefusis

Flushing

School

Trefusis Point

FALMOUTH

Prince of Wales Pier

Inner Harbour

Queens Wharf

Northern Wharf

Empire Wharf

Fish Strand Quay

King's Wharf

Western Wharf

FALMOUTH DOCKS

Ferry to St. Mawes

Duchy Wharf

North Quay
Maritime Museum
Custom House Quay

County Wharf

No. 4 Dock

No. 3 Dock

No. 1 Dock

Qn. Elizabeth Dock

Eastern Breakwater

PORT PENDENNIS

FALMOUTH

THE DELL

Falmouth Hotel

Ships & Castles Leisure Pool

Middle Point

MELVILL ROAD

Princess Pavilion

Castle Beach

Pendennis Castle

Tunnel Beach

Coastguard Lookout

Crab Quay

Gyllyngvase Beach

Mary Gardens

PENDENNIS POINT

anpool Point

A - Z INDEX TO STREETS
with Postcodes

The Index includes some names for which there is insufficient space on the maps. These names are indicated by an * and are followed by the nearest adjoining thoroughfare.

FALMOUTH

Acacia Rd TR11	12 B2
Albany Pl TR11	12 D4
Albany Rd TR11	12 D4
Albert Cotts TR11	13 E4
Arundell Grn TR11	12 B2
Arwenack Av TR11	13 E4
Arwenack St TR11	13 E4
Ashfield Estate TR11	12 B2
Ashfield Rd TR11	12 B2
Ashfield Villas TR11	12 B2
Avenue Rd TR11	13 E5
Bar La TR11	13 E5
Bar Rd TR11	13 F5
Bar Ter TR11	13 F4
Bassett Pl TR11	12 D2
Bay Ct TR11	13 E5
Bay View Cres TR11	13 F5
Beacon Cres TR11	12 D3
Beacon Rd TR11	12 D2
Beacon St TR11	12 D2
Beacon Ter TR11	12 D2
Beech Clo TR11	12 C3
Beech Rd TR11	12 C3
Belmont Rd TR11	12 D4
Berkeley Cotts TR11	12 D3
Berkeley Hill TR11	12 D3
*Berkeley Path, Berkeley Hill TR11	12 D3
Berkeley Vale TR11	12 D3
Berryman Cres TR11	12 C5
Bickland Hill TR11	12 A3
Bickland Vale TR11	12 A3
Bickland Water Rd TR11	12 A3
Boscawen Rd TR11	12 D6
Boscundle Av TR11	12 B6
Bosloggas Mews TR11	13 F4
Boslowick Clo TR11	12 B5
Boslowick Rd TR11	12 B6
Bosmeor Clo TR11	12 A5
Bosmeor Rd TR11	12 A5
Bowles Rd TR11	12 C2
Brook Pl TR11	12 D4
Brook Rd TR11	12 C4
Brook St TR11	12 D4
Budock Ter TR11	12 D4
Cambeltown Way TR11	13 E4
Cambridge Pl TR11	12 D5
Captains Walk TR11	12 C5
Carrick Rd TR11	12 B6
Castle Dri TR11	13 G5
Castle Hill TR11	13 F5
Charles Av TR11	12 B5
Chestnut Clo TR11	12 C3
Church St TR11	13 E3
Church Way TR11	12 B4
Clairmont Cotts TR11	12 D3
Clare Ter TR11	13 E4
Claremont Ter*, Beacon St TR11	12 D2
Cliff Rd TR11	13 E5
Clifton Cres TR11	12 C4
Clifton Pl TR11	12 D4
Clifton Ter TR11	12 D4
Colworth Av TR11	12 C4
Conway Clo TR11	12 B3
Conway Gdns TR11	12 A3
Conway Rd TR11	12 A3
Coventry Rd TR11	13 E1
Crossways TR11	12 B5

Daveys Clo TR11	12 B6
De Pass Gdns TR11	13 F5
De Pass Rd TR11	13 F5
Diana Clo TR11	12 B5
Dracaena Av TR11	12 B2
Dracaena Pl TR11	12 C3
Duncannon Dri TR11	12 C4
East Rise TR11	12 C5
Eastwood Rd TR10	12 A1
Elowen Clo TR11	12 A5
Emslie Rd TR11	13 E5
Erisey Ter TR11	12 D3
Esperanza Ct TR11	12 C2
Fairfield Rd TR11	12 C3
Falmouth Rd TR10	12 A1
Fawkener Clo TR11	12 B4
Fenwick Rd TR11	12 D5
Ferndale Rd TR11	12 C5
Florence Pl TR11	13 E4
Florence Ter TR11	12 D4
Fox La TR11	13 E4
Foxs La TR11	13 E5
Frankland Clo TR11	12 C4
Freeman Collins Dri TR11	12 B3
Frobisher Ter TR11	12 D2
Frost Ct TR11	12 B3
Garden Mdw TR11	12 B4
Glasney Rd TR11	12 C2
Godolphin Rd TR11	12 C2
Greenbank TR11	12 D2
Grenville Clo TR11	12 C3
Grenville Rd TR11	12 C3
Grove Pl TR11	13 E4
Grovehill Cres TR11	13 E4
Grovehill Dri TR11	13 E5
Gyllyng St TR11	13 E4
Gyllyngvase Hill TR11	13 E5
Gyllyngvase Rd TR11	13 E5
Gyllyngvase Ter TR11	13 E5
Harbour Ter TR11	12 D3
Hawkins Way TR11	12 D4
Hayman Way TR11	12 B2
High St TR11	12 D3
Highfield Rd TR11	12 C3
Hill Head TR10	12 A1
Hillside Meadow TR10	12 A1
Hillside Rd TR11	12 B5
Hulls La TR11	13 E4
Jubilee Rd TR11	12 D3
Kelly Rd TR11	12 B3
Kerensa Grn TR11	12 B2
Kersey Rd TR11	13 E1
Killigrew St TR11	12 D4
Kimberley Pk Rd TR11	12 C3
Kimberley Pl TR11	12 D4
Kings Av TR11	12 C4
Laburnum Clo TR11	12 B2
Laburnum Dri TR11	12 C2
Lambs La TR11	12 B2
Langton Rd TR11	12 C2
Langton Ter TR11	12 D2
Lansdowne Rd TR11	13 E5
Link Clo TR11	12 B4
Lister Hill TR11	12 D4
Lister St TR11	12 D4
Longfield TR11	12 A4
Lowenek Clo TR11	12 B2
Madeira Walk TR11	12 D5
Manor Clo TR11	12 A3
Manor Cres TR11	12 A3
Manor Rd TR11	12 B3
Margaret Pl TR11	12 C4
Market St TR11	13 E3
Marlborough Av TR11	12 C5
Marlborough Clo TR11	12 C5
Marlborough Ct TR11	12 C4
Marlborough Cres TR11	12 C4
Marlborough Gro TR11	12 C5
Marlborough Rd TR11	12 C5
Mayfield Rd TR11	12 C3
Meadowbank Rd TR11	12 C2

Meadowside Rd TR11	12 B5
Mearwood La TR11	12 B3
Melvill Cres TR11	13 E5
Melvill Rd TR11	12 D5
Merrill Pl TR11	12 D4
Messack Clo TR11	12 B5
Mongleath Av TR11	12 B4
Mongleath Clo TR11	12 B5
Mongleath Rd TR11	12 A4
Mount Stephens La TR11	12 B3
New St TR11	13 E4
Norfolk Rd TR11	12 D4
North Par TR11	12 C2
Noweth Pl TR11	12 B2
Oakfield Rd TR11	12 B2
Old Hill TR11	12 C2
Old Hill Cres TR11	12 C2
Packet Quays TR11	12 D3
Park Cres TR11	12 C3
Park Hill TR11	12 D4
Park Rise TR11	12 C3
Park Ter TR11	12 C4
Pellew Clo TR11	12 C2
Pellew Rd TR11	12 C3
Penarrow Clo TR11	12 B6
Penarth Rd TR11	12 D2
Pendarves Rd TR11	12 C2
Pendennis Rise TR11	13 F5
Pendennis Rd TR11	13 F5
Pengarth Rise TR11	12 C5
Pengarth Rd TR11	12 C5
Pengelly Pl TR11	12 B2
Penhale Rd TR11	12 B6
Penmere Cres TR11	12 C4
Penmere Hill TR11	12 C4
Penmere Pl TR11	12 C4
Pennance Rd TR11	12 D5
Penrose Rd TR11	12 C3
Penryn By-Pass TR11	12 A1
Penvean La TR11	12 B3
Penwerris La TR11	12 D2
Penwerris Ter TR11	12 D2
Pit Meadow TR11	12 B4
Polventon Clo TR11	12 B3
Polwithen Rd TR11	12 C3
Porhan Grn TR11	12 B2
Portland Gdns TR11	12 C4
Prince St TR11	12 D3
Prislow Clo TR11	12 B5
Prislow Fields TR11	12 B5
Prislow La TR11	12 A5
Prospect Pl*, Beacon St TR11	12 D2
Quarry Hill TR11	12 D3
Quay Hill TR11	13 E4
Queen Anne Gdns TR11	12 B4
Queen Mary Ct TR11	12 D6
Queen Mary Rd TR11	12 D6
Robert Hichens Rd TR11	12 C2
Roscarrack Clo TR11	12 A5
St Anthony Way TR11	12 D5
St Peters Rd TR11	12 D1
St Smithwick Way TR11	13 F4
Sea View Rd TR11	12 D5
Shelburne Rd TR11	12 B4
Silverdale Rd TR11	12 C5
Spernen Wyn Rd TR11	12 D5
Stracey Rd TR11	13 E5
Stratton Ter TR11	12 D2
Swanpool Hill TR11	12 D5
Swanpool Rd TR11	12 C6
Swanpool St TR11	13 E4
Swanvale Rd TR11	12 B4
Symons Hill TR11	12 D2
The Beacon Est TR11	12 D3
The Causeway TR11	12 B4
The Gluyas TR11	12 B6
The Moor TR11	12 D3
The Nurseries TR11	12 A3
Theydon Rd TR11	12 C4
Tinners Walk TR11	13 F4

Trecarne TR11	12 B2
Tredova Cres TR11	12 D6
Tredynas Rd TR11	13 G5
Tredyson Pl TR11	12 C4
Trefusis Rd, Falmouth TR11	12 B6
Trefusis Rd, Flushing TR11	13 E2
Tregenver Rd TR11	12 C3
Tregenver Villas TR11	12 C3
Tregoniggie TR11	12 A3
Tregoniggie Ind Est TR11	12 A4
Tregothnan Rd TR11	12 C3
Tregullow Rd TR11	12 B2
Tregunter Mews TR11	13 F4
Trehidy Ter TR11	12 C1
Trelawney Av TR11	13 E5
Trelawney Rd TR11	12 D4
Trelissick Rd TR11	12 B3
Tremanor Way TR11	12 A3
Tresahar Rd TR11	12 D5
Tresawle Rd TR11	12 C2
Tresawna Ter TR11	12 D3
Tresco Pl TR11	12 C3
Trescobeas Rd TR11	12 A3
Tresillian Rd TR11	12 C2
Trevarth Rd TR11	12 B3
Trevaylor Rd TR11	12 B3
Treveglos Rd TR11	12 B6
Treventon Rise TR11	12 C3
Treventon Clo TR11	12 B3
Treverbyn Rd TR11	12 B6
Trevethan Clo TR11	12 D3
Trevethan Hill*, Beacon St TR11	12 D2
Trevethan Rd TR11	12 D3
Trevithick Rd TR11	12 B3
Tuke Clo TR11	12 B2
Turnaware Rd TR11	12 B6
Union Corner TR11	12 A2
Union Rd TR11	12 A2
Venton Rd TR11	12 B3
Vernon Pl TR11	12 D3
Waterloo Rd TR11	12 D4
Webber St TR11	12 D3
Weller Ct TR11	12 D5
Wellington Pl TR11	12 D3
Wellington Ter TR11	12 D4
West Rise TR11	12 B5
West St TR11	12 D4
Western Ter TR11	12 D4
Windsor Ct TR11	12 D4
Windsor Ter TR11	12 D4
Wodehouse Ter TR11	13 E4
Wood Clo TR11	13 E4
Wood Dri TR11	13 E4
Wood La TR11	12 D5
Woodlane Cres TR11	12 D4

MYLOR BRIDGE

Bells Hill TR11	10 B1
Bissom Rd TR10	10 B3
Bonython Clo TR11	10 C2
Broads La TR11	10 A1
Church Rd TR11	10 C3
Cogos Pk TR11	10 B1
Comfort Rd TR11	10 B2
Eglos Meadow TR11	10 C1
Lemon Hill TR11	10 B2
Lemon Hill Gdns TR11	10 B2
Meadow Bank TR11	10 C1
New Row TR11	10 B2
Olivey Pl TR11	10 B1
Parc Peneglos TR11	10 C1
Passage Hill TR11	10 C2
Penmorvah TR11	10 A3
Penoweth TR11	10 B3
Pillars Rd TR11	10 C3

Street	Postcode	Ref
Rosehill	TR11	10 B3
Saltbox Clo	TR11	10 C3
Saltbox Rd	TR11	10 B3
Springfield Pk	TR11	10 B1
The Close	TR11	10 B1
Trevellan Rd	TR11	10 C2
Waterings Rd	TR11	10 B2
Willow Clo	TR11	10 B2

PENRYN

Street	Postcode	Ref
Alderwood Parc	TR10	11 D2
Andrewartha Rd	TR10	11 D2
Annear Rd	TR10	11 C3
Antron Hill	TR10	11 A3
Antron La	TR10	11 A3
Antron Way	TR10	11 A3
Audierne*, Higher Market St	TR10	11 E2
Belhay	TR10	11 E1
Bickland Vale	TR11	11 F4
Bissom	TR10	11 F1
Bissom Rd	TR10	11 F1
Bohelland Rise	TR10	11 E1
Bohelland Rd	TR10	11 E1
Bohelland Way	TR10	11 E1
Bohill	TR10	11 F2
Broad St	TR10	11 E2
Bronescombe Clo	TR10	11 E3
Brook Pl	TR10	11 E2
Browns Hill	TR10	11 D1
Carnsew Clo	TR10	11 A2
Challacombe Gdns	TR10	11 E1
Chapel La	TR10	11 E2
Charter Ct	TR10	11 F2
Church Hill	TR10	11 F1
Church Rd, Mabe Burnthouse	TR10	11 A4
Church Rd, Penryn	TR10	11 E1
College Hill	TR10	11 E3
Commercial Rd	TR10	11 E2
Conway Rd	TR11	11 F4
Coronation Cotts	TR10	11 A3
Cunningham Pk	TR10	11 A2
Dunstan Clo	TR10	11 E2
Dunvegan Rd	TR10	11 D1
Durgan La	TR10	11 D1
Eastwood Rd	TR10	11 F2
Erow Glas	TR10	11 E1
Eston Clo	TR10	11 A3
Falmouth Rd	TR10	11 F2
Fox Stanton Dri	TR10	11 F3
Gills Clo	TR10	11 C3
Glasney Pl	TR10	11 E2
Glasney Ter	TR10	11 E2
Glen View	TR10	11 C1
Green La	TR10	11 C2
Green Lane Clo	TR10	11 D2
Greenwood Cres	TR10	11 C1
Greenwood Rd	TR10	11 C1
Gweal Darras	TR10	11 A2
Harbour View	TR10	11 D1
Helston Rd	TR10	11 D2
Higher Market St	TR10	11 E2
Highland Pk	TR10	11 D1
Hill Head	TR10	11 E3
Hillhead Rd	TR11	11 D4
Hillside Mdw	TR10	11 F3
Jacks Clo	TR10	11 F3
Jennings Rd	TR10	11 B3
Kergilliack Rd	TR11	11 E4
Kernick Ind Est	TR10	11 B2
Kernick Rd	TR10	11 A3
Lanaton Rd	TR10	11 C2
Little Oaks	TR10	11 C3
Love La	TR10	11 F1
Lower St	TR10	11 E2
Manor Clo	TR11	11 F4
Manor Rd	TR11	11 F4
New St	TR10	11 E2
Oakland Park	TR11	11 E4
Old Well Gdns	TR10	11 E1
Packsaddle	TR10	11 C1
Parc-An-Challow	TR10	11 D2
Parc Bower	TR10	11 E3
Parkengue	TR10	11 C2
Penlea Rd	TR10	11 C2
Penryn By-Pass	TR10	11 B3
Pentire Rd	TR10	11 C2
Penvale Cres	TR10	11 C2
Penvale Dri	TR10	11 D1
Penvean Clo	TR10	11 A3
Permarin Rd	TR10	11 E2
Polsethow	TR10	11 D2
Poltair Rd	TR10	11 D2
Poltisko Rd	TR10	11 D2
Poltisko Ter	TR10	11 D2
Polwithen Rd	TR10	11 D2
Praze Mead	TR10	11 E1
Quay Hill	TR10	11 F2
Round Ring	TR10	11 E1
St Gluvias Parc	TR10	11 E1
St Gluvias St	TR10	11 E2
St Thomas St	TR10	11 E2
Saracen Clo	TR10	11 E2
Saracen Cres	TR10	11 E2
Saracen Pl	TR10	11 E2
Saracen Way	TR10	11 D2
Shute Meadow	TR10	11 D2
Slades La	TR10	11 D2
South View	TR10	11 E1
Spargo Ct	TR10	11 A3
Station Rd	TR10	11 D1
Summer Heath	TR10	11 B2
The Nurseries	TR11	11 F4
The Praze	TR10	11 D1
Trekeen Rd	TR10	11 D2
Treliever Rd, Mabe Burnthouse	TR10	11 A2
Treliever Rd, Penryn	TR10	11 D1
Tremanor Way	TR11	11 F4
Trenarth	TR10	11 E2
Trescobeas Rd	TR11	11 F4
Tresooth La	TR10	11 D1
Trevance	TR10	11 C2
Treverbyn Rise	TR10	11 C2
Trewarton Rd	TR10	11 C1
Truro Hill	TR10	11 E1
Truro La	TR10	11 E2
Union Rd	TR11	11 E3
West End	TR10	11 D1
West End Clo	TR10	11 D1
West St	TR10	11 D2
Western Pl	TR10	11 D1
Woodland Av	TR10	11 C3
Woodland Rise	TR10	11 D3
Woodside	TR10	11 D3
Woodview	TR10	11 D3
Woodway	TR10	11 D3

ST. MAWES

Street	Postcode	Ref
Bohella Rd	TR2	10 B5
Buckeys La	TR2	10 C6
Carrick Way	TR2	10 C5
Castle Dri	TR2	10 A6
Chapel Ter	TR2	10 B6
Church Hill	TR2	10 B6
Commercial Rd	TR2	10 B6
Freshwater La	TR2	10 C5
Grove Hill	TR2	10 B5
Hillhead	TR2	10 C5
Kings Rd	TR2	10 B6
Lower Castle Rd	TR2	10 A6
Marine Parade	TR2	10 B6
Newton Pk	TR2	10 B5
Newton Rd	TR2	10 B5
Pedn Moran	TR2	10 C5
Pen Brea Clo	TR2	10 C5
Penruan La	TR2	10 C5
Percuil View	TR2	10 C5
Place View Rd	TR2	10 B5
Polvarth Rd	TR2	10 B4
Porth View	TR2	10 C5
Riviera La	TR2	10 B6
St Austell Row	TR2	10 C5
Sea View Cres	TR2	10 B5
The Quay	TR2	10 B6
The Square	TR2	10 C5
Tredenham Rd	TR2	10 C5
Trelawney Rd	TR2	10 B5
Upper Castle Rd	TR2	10 A6
Waterloo Clo	TR2	10 C5

TRURO

Street	Postcode	Ref
Adelaide Ter*, Crescent Rd	TR1	5 E4
Agar Ct	TR1	5 G4
Agar Rd	TR1	5 G4
Albany Rd	TR1	4 C4
Albert Pl	TR1	5 E5
Alma Rd	TR1	4 C4
Alverton Ct	TR1	5 G3
Alverton Ter	TR1	5 G3
Arch Hill	TR1	5 E6
Arundell Pl	TR1	5 F5
Arworthal Meadows	TR3	8 B4
Ashley Rd	TR1	5 E5
Avondale Rd	TR1	4 D4
Back Quay	TR1	5 F4
Barrack La	TR1	5 F5
Barton Meadow	TR1	4 D3
Bedruthan Av	TR1	5 G2
Beechwood Gdns	TR1	5 H2
Behenna Dri	TR1	4 B4
Belmont Ter	TR3	9 E4
Benson Rd	TR1	5 E3
Berveth Clo	TR3	6 C2
Bishop Temple Rd	TR1	5 H3
Bishops Clo	TR1	5 F2
Bissoe Rd	TR3	8 C1
Blackberry Way	TR1	5 H3
Bodmin Rd	TR1	5 G2
Boscawen St	TR1	5 F4
Bosvean Gdns	TR1	4 D4
Bosvigo La	TR1	4 D4
Bosvigo Rd	TR1	5 E4
Brewers Rd	TR1	5 H3
Broad St	TR1	5 G3
Burley Clo	TR1	5 F5
Calenick St	TR1	5 F4
Campfield Hill	TR1	5 F4
Carclew St	TR1	5 F5
Carclew Ter	TR3	9 E4
Carew Pole Clo	TR1	5 G5
Carew Rd	TR1	5 E3
Carey Park	TR1	5 E5
Carlton Rd	TR3	7 C4
Carlyon Clo	TR3	6 C2
Carlyon Rd	TR1	5 E3
Carnon Cres	TR3	9 F2
Carnon Ter	TR3	9 E4
Carrine Rd	TR1	4 A5
Carvoza Rd	TR1	5 F3
Castle Rise	TR1	5 E3
Castle St	TR1	5 F4
Cathedral La	TR1	5 F4
Cathedral Vw	TR1	5 E2
Chainwalk Dri	TR1	5 E3
Chapel Hill	TR1	4 D5
Chapel Pl	TR1	5 F5
Chapel Row	TR1	5 F5
Chapel Ter	TR3	9 E4
Charles St	TR1	5 F4
Chellew Rd	TR1	5 H3
Chirgwin Rd	TR1	5 G4
Church Rd	TR3	8 B5
Church Ter	TR3	9 E4
Chy Hwel	TR1	5 H3
Chycoose Pk	TR3	9 H5
Chyreen La	TR3	7 A6
Chyvelah Ope	TR3	6 E3
Chyvelah Rd	TR3	6 B2
Chyvelah Vale	TR1	6 E2
Chyvogue La	TR3	8 A4
Chyvogue Mdw	TR3	8 A4
City Rd	TR1	5 E4
Cleswyth	TR1	4 C4
Coldrose Ct	TR1	4 D5
College Rd	TR1	6 E2
College Way	TR1	6 E2
Comprigney Clo	TR1	4 D3
Comprigney Hill	TR1	4 D3
Coombes La	TR1	5 F4
Coosebean La	TR1	4 C3
Copes Gdns	TR1	5 E3
Cornish Cres	TR1	4 B4
Cornubia Clo	TR1	5 H2
Cotsland Rd	TR1	5 H3
Courtney Rd	TR1	5 E3
Cove Hill	TR3	8 A5
Cowling Rd	TR3	9 F1
Crescent Gdns	TR1	4 D4
Crescent Rise	TR1	4 D4
Crescent Rd	TR1	5 E4
Cryon View	TR1	4 A4
Curlew Pk Ind Est	TR3	6 B2
Cyril Rd	TR1	5 E3
Daniell Ct	TR1	5 E5
Daniell Rd	TR1	5 E5
Daniell St	TR1	5 E5
Daubuz Clo	TR1	5 E3
Daubuz Ct	TR1	5 E3
David Penhaligon Way	TR1	5 F5
Deeble Clo	TR3	6 C2
Dereham*, Chapel Hill	TR1	5 E4
Devoran La	TR3	9 E4
Dobbs La	TR1	4 D4
Dudman Rd	TR1	4 C4
Duke St	TR1	5 F4
Eastland Clo	TR1	5 H4
Edward St	TR1	5 E4
Edwards Rd	TR3	9 E4
Eliot Rd	TR1	5 E3
Elm Ct	TR1	5 F3
Elm Ct Gdns	TR1	5 F3
Enys Clo	TR1	5 E3
Enys Rd	TR1	5 E3
Epworth Clo	TR1	5 G4
Evea Clo	TR1	4 A5
Fairmantle St	TR1	5 F5
Falmouth Rd	TR1	5 E6
Ferris Town	TR1	5 E4
Forth Noweth	TR3	9 E1
Frances St	TR1	5 E4
Furniss Clo*, St Austell St	TR1	5 G4
Galland Rd	TR1	4 C4
Gas Hill	TR1	5 G6
George St	TR1	5 E4
Gig La	TR3	9 F1
Glenthorne Rd	TR3	6 B2
Gloweth Vw	TR1	4 A4
Glyn Way	TR3	6 D2
Green Clo	TR1	5 E5
Green La	TR1	5 E5
Green St	TR1	5 F4
Greenbank Rd	TR3	8 D4
Greenwith Clo	TR1	5 E5
Greenwith Hill	TR3	8 A1
Greenwith Rd	TR3	8 A3
Gregor Rd	TR1	5 H3
Grenna La	TR3	8 A1
Grenville Rd	TR1	5 E3
Gwarnick Rd	TR1	5 E4
Gwendroc Clo	TR1	5 F5
Halvarras Pk	TR3	7 C6
Halvarras Rd	TR3	7 C5
Halwyn Pl	TR1	5 E5
Harbour Vw	TR1	5 H6
Harcourt Clo	TR1	4 C4
Harrison Ter*, The Crescent	TR1	4 D4
Harvey Rd	TR1	5 G6
Hawthorn Way	TR3	6 B2
Hendra Barton	TR1	5 E3
Hendra La	TR1	5 E3
Hendra Vean	TR1	5 E3
High Cross	TR1	5 F4
Higher Newham La	TR1	5 G6
Higher Redannick	TR1	5 E5
Higher Trehaverne	TR1	5 E3
Highertown	TR1	4 B4
Hill Crest Av	TR1	4 D4
Holly Clo	TR3	6 B2
Holywell Rd	TR3	7 B5
Hugus Rd	TR3	6 C2
Hunkin Clo	TR1	5 F3

Hurland Rd TR1	5 F5	Newmills La TR1	4 C2	*Robartes Ct,
Huthnance Clo TR1	5 H3	Newquay Rd TR1	5 H1	Redannick La TR1
Hyne Corfe Gdns TR1	4 C4	Northfield Dri TR1	5 F5	Rosedale Rd TR1
Infirmary Hill TR1	5 F5	Nursery Clo TR1	5 F3	Rosevalley TR3
James Pl TR1	5 G4	Oak La TR1	4 A3	Rosewin Row TR1
John St TR1	5 E4	Oak Way TR1	5 F3	St Aubyns Rd TR1
Jubilee Rd TR1	6 B3	Old Bridge St TR1	5 F4	St Austell St TR1
Keeble Pk TR3	8 C3	Old Carnon Hill TR3	8 D3	St Clement St TR1
Kenna Park TR1	4 B4	Old Coach Rd TR3	7 B5	St Clements Clo TR1
Kenwyn Church Rd TR1	5 E3	Old Falmouth Rd TR1	5 E6	St Clements Hill TR1
Kenwyn Clo TR1	5 E2	Old Tram Rd TR3	9 G5	St Clements Parc TR1
Kenwyn Hill TR1	4 D2	Orchard Clo TR1	4 C4	St Dominic St TR1
Kenwyn Rd TR1	5 E3	Pargos La TR1	5 G4	St Georges Rd TR1
Kenwyn St TR1	5 E4	Park An Gwarry TR3	9 F2	St Johns Ter TR3
Kerley Gro TR1	4 B4	Park View TR1	5 F5	St Keyne Clo TR1
Kerris Gro TR1	4 D3	Park View Clo TR1	9 F2	St Mary's St TR1
Kestle Dri TR1	4 C4	Parkancreeg TR3	9 E2	St Nicholas St TR1
King St TR1	5 F4	Parkvedras*,		St Pirans Hill TR3
Kingsley Clo TR1	6 E3	Chapel Hill TR1	5 E4	St Thomas Clo TR1
Kirby Rd TR1	4 C4	Pascoe Clo TR3	6 C2	Salisbury Rd TR1
Knights Hill TR1	5 E2	Pauls Row TR1	5 F3	Sampson Way TR3
Knights Meadow TR3	9 E2	Pauls Ter TR1	5 F3	School Hill TR3
Knoll Pk TR1	5 H4	Penair Cres TR1	5 H2	School La TR1
Lamellyn Dri TR1	4 A4	Penair Vw TR1	5 H4	Seymour Clo TR3
Lanyon Rd TR3	7 B5	Pencarrick Clo TR1	4 D2	Silver Hill TR3
Leap Park TR3	6 B3	Pendale Sq TR1	5 E5	Silver Way TR3
Lemon Mews TR1	5 F4	Pendarves Rd TR1	5 F3	Smithy La TR3
Lemon Quay TR1	5 F4	Pendeen Clo TR3	6 C2	Springfield Way TR3
Lemon St TR1	5 F5	Pendeen Rd,		Staggy La TR3
Lighterage Hill TR1	5 G6	Threemilestone TR3	6 C2	Station Rd,
Linley Clo TR3	6 C2	Pendeen Rd, Truro TR1	5 G6	Perranwell Station TR3
Little Castle St TR1	5 F4	Pendrea Wood TR1	4 C4	Station Rd, Truro TR1
Lodge Dri TR1	5 H2	Pengarth Clo TR1	5 F6	Stokes Rd TR1
Lowen Way TR3	6 B2	Pengelly Way TR3	6 C2	Strangways Ter TR1
Lower Comprigney TR1	4 D3	Penhaligon Ct TR1	5 G3	Stratton Ter TR1
Lower Hugus Rd TR3	6 B3	Penhalls Way TR3	7 C5	Stretyn TR3
Lower Polstain Rd TR3	6 C3	Penlee Villas TR3	7 C5	Sunningdale TR1
Lower Redannick TR1	5 E4	Penmorvah Rd TR1	5 H2	Tabernacle St TR1
Lukes Clo TR1	5 H3	Penpol Hill TR3	9 H4	Tarrandean La TR3
Lychgate Dri TR1	5 E2	Pensilva Rd TR1	5 H2	The Avenue TR1
Malabar Rd TR1	4 B4	Penventinnie La TR1	4 A3	The Close TR1
Malpas Rd TR1	5 G4	Penwerris Rd TR1	4 B4	The Courtyard TR1
Manor Gdns TR1	5 G3	Penwethers La TR1	4 B5	The Crescent TR1
Manse Rd TR3	9 F1	Perran Clo TR3	9 E4	The Forge TR3
Meadow Clo TR1	6 F3	Point Rd TR3	9 F3	The Leas TR1
Meadow La TR1	5 F6	Polruan Rd TR1	5 G6	The Leats TR1
Merrick Av TR1	5 G3	Polstain Cres TR3	6 D2	The Spires TR1
Merrifield Clo TR1	5 E4	Polstain Rd TR3	6 D2	Threemilestone Ind Est
Midway Dri TR1	5 G3	Poltisco Clo TR1	5 G5	TR3
Mill Race Path TR1	5 F2	Polwhele Rd TR1	5 H2	Tre-El-Verne Clo TR1
Mitchell Hill TR1	5 G4	Princes St TR1	5 F4	Trebartha Clo TR1
Monterey Gdns TN1	5 G3	Prospect Gdns TR1	5 G3	Trecarne Clo TR1
Moresk Clo TR1	5 F3	Prospect Pl TR1	5 F3	Tredrea Gdns TR3
Moresk Gdns TR1	5 F3	Pydar St TR1	5 E3	Trefusis Clo TR1
Moresk Rd TR1	5 F3	Quay Rd TR3	9 E4	Tregavethan View TR3
Morlaix Av TR1	5 E6	Quay St TR1	5 F4	Tregear Gdns TR1
Mount Agar Rd TR3	9 E2	Quenchwell Rd TR3	9 F1	Tregolls Clo TR1
Mount Pleasant Rd TR3	6 D2	Rashleigh Vale TR1	5 G4	Tregolls Rd TR1
Murdoch Clo TR1	5 G3	Redannick Ct*,		Tregothan Rd TR1
Nancemere Rd TR1	5 G2	Redannick La TR1	5 E4	Tregurra La TR1
Nansavallon Rd TR1	4 A4	Redannick Cres TR1	5 E5	Trehaverne La TR1
New Bridge St TR1	5 F4	Redannick La TR1	5 E5	Trelander Barton TR1
Newbridge La TR1	4 A5	Richards Cres TR1	4 B4	Trelander East TR1
Newbridge Way TR1	4 A5	Richmond Hill TR1	5 E4	Trelander Highway TR1
Newham Est TR1	5 F5	Richmond Pl TR1	5 E4	Trelander North TR1
Newham Ind Est TR1	**5 G6**	Richmond Ter TR1	5 E4	Trelander Path TR1
Newham Rd TR1	5 G5	River St TR1	5 F4	Trelander South TR1
Newmills Clo TR1	4 D2	Riverside Vw TR1	5 G5	Trelawne Clo TR3

Redannick La TR1	5 E4	Trelawne Rd TR3	9 E2
Rosedale Rd TR1	5 E3	Trelawney Rd TR1	5 E3
Rosevalley TR3	6 C3	Treleaver Way TR1	4 C5
Rosewin Row TR1	5 F4	**Treliske Ind Est TR1**	**4 A3**
St Aubyns Rd TR1	5 F5	Treliske La TR1	4 B4
St Austell St TR1	5 G4	Tremayne Clo TR3	9 E4
St Clement St TR1	5 F4	Tremayne Rd TR1	5 E3
St Clements Clo TR1	5 H4	Tremorvah Barton TR1	5 G3
St Clements Hill TR1	5 H4	Tremorvah Ct TR1	5 G3
St Clements Parc TR1	5 H4	Tremorvah Cres TR1	5 G3
St Dominic St TR1	5 E4	Tremorvah Wood La	
St Georges Rd TR1	4 D3	TR1	5 G3
St Johns Ter TR3	9 E4	Trenerry Clo TR1	5 G2
St Keyne Clo TR1	5 F2	Trennick La TR1	5 G4
St Mary's St TR1	5 F4	Tresawls Av TR1	4 A4
St Nicholas St TR1	5 F4	Tresawls Rd TR1	4 A4
St Pirans Hill TR3	8 A5	Treseders Gdns TR1	5 F3
St Thomas Clo TR1	4 B4	Trethowan Heights TR1	4 C5
Salisbury Rd TR1	5 E5	Trevanion Clo TR1	4 C4
Sampson Way TR3	6 C2	Trevaylor Clo TR1	5 G2
School Hill TR3	8 A5	Trevean Rd TR1	4 B4
School La TR1	5 E5	Trevelva Rd TR1	5 G6
Seymour Clo TR3	6 B2	Treverbyn Rd TR1	5 G2
Silver Hill TR3	8 A3	Trevethenick Rd TR1	5 G5
Silver Way TR3	6 C3	Trevithick Clo TR1	5 G3
Smithy La TR3	9 E2	Trevithick Rd TR1	5 G2
Springfield Way TR3	6 C3	Trevose Rd TR1	4 B4
Staggy La TR3	9 F2	Trewidden Clo TR1	5 H3
Station Rd,		Trewidden Ct TR1	5 H4
Perranwell Station TR3	8 B3	Trewinnard Gro TR1	5 E3
Station Rd, Truro TR1	4 D4	Trewinnard Rd TR3	8 A5
Stokes Rd TR1	5 E3	Treworder Rd TR1	5 E5
Strangways Ter TR1	5 F5	Treworthal Rd TR3	8 A5
Stratton Ter TR1	5 E4	Treyew Rd TR1	4 C4
Stretyn TR3	9 F1	Truro Vean Ter TR1	5 F4
Sunningdale TR1	4 D4	Union Pl TR1	5 F4
Tabernacle St TR1	5 F4	Union St TR1	5 F4
Tarrandean La TR3	8 C3	Upland Clo TR1	5 H3
The Avenue TR1	5 G3	Upland Cres TR1	5 G3
The Close TR1	5 H2	Uplands Vean TR1	5 H3
The Courtyard TR1	5 F5	Upper School La TR1	5 E5
The Crescent TR1	4 D4	Upper Tredrea TR3	8 A5
The Forge TR3	9 F1	Valley Clo TR1	4 B5
The Leas TR1	5 G3	Valley La TR3	9 F1
The Leats TR1	5 F4	Valley View Dri TR1	4 B4
The Spires TR1	5 E2	Victoria Gdns TR3	6 C2
Threemilestone Ind Est		Victoria Rd TR3	6 C3
TR3	**6 A2**	Victoria Sq TR1	5 F4
Tre-El-Verne Clo TR1	4 C4	**Walsingham Pl TR1**	5 F4
Trebartha Clo TR1	5 H4	Waterloo TR1	5 G4
Trecarne Clo TR1	5 H4	West Park TR3	8 A4
Tredrea Gdns TR3	8 A5	Westmoor Cres TR3	8 A4
Trefusis Clo TR1	5 H4	Wheal Jane Mdws TR3	6 B2
Tregavethan View TR3	6 B2	Whitley Clo TR1	5 H4
Tregear Gdns TR1	5 F4	Wilkes Way TR1	5 F4
Tregolls Clo TR1	5 H3	William St TR1	5 F5
Tregolls Rd TR1	5 G4	Wood La TR1	5 F5
Tregothan Rd TR1	5 G6	Woodland Ct TR1	5 G3
Tregurra La TR1	5 G2	Woodland Heights TR1	5 G3
Trehaverne La TR1	5 E3	Woon La TR3	9 F1
Trelander Barton TR1	5 G4		
Trelander East TR1	5 H4		
Trelander Highway TR1	5 G4		
Trelander North TR1	5 H4		
Trelander Path TR1	5 H4		
Trelander South TR1	5 H4		
Trelawne Clo TR3	9 E2		